Deal

RACISM

by Jane Lacey

Illustrated by Venitia Dean

W

FRANKLIN WATTS

Franklin Watts
Published in paperback in Great Britain in 2019 by The Watts Publishing Group

Copyright © The Watts Publishing Group, 2017
The text in this book was originally published in the series 'How can I deal with'

Credits
Series Editor: Sarah Peutrill
Series Design: Collaborate

ISBN 978 1 4451 5790 0

Printed in China

Franklin Watts
An imprint of
Hachette Children's Group
Part of The Watts Publishing Group
Carmelite House
50 Victoria Embankment
London EC4Y 0DZ

An Hachette UK Company
www.hachette.co.uk

www.franklinwatts.co.uk

Contents

I'M NEW IN THIS COUNTRY AND AT SCHOOL

Kwame is a new boy at school. He has just arrived from Ghana. He's learning English and he's shy because he can't speak English very well yet.

Marek is Kwame's friend

Kwame is in my class. I'm from Poland and I know what it feels like to be new and learning a new language. I want to be Kwame's friend but I don't know if he wants to be mine.

Kwame's Story

I'm learning English but the other children talk so quickly! They laugh when I pull a face if I don't understand them. I was clever at my school in Ghana and got top marks. But I don't feel clever here.

I want to play football. I was captain of my class team in Ghana. When the kids were choosing a team at playtime, one of them pointed at me and said, "Don't choose him, he's stupid." I understood him when he said that!

Kwame

5

The children are being unfair to Kwame by not giving him a chance. He can:

★ talk to his mum and dad
★ tell them not being good at English makes him feel shy and not clever
★ say he finds it difficult to make friends
★ say he wants to play football!

what Kwame did

I talked to Dad. He talked to Miss Everard. She helped me tell the children about my school in Ghana. I showed them photos of me playing football! Now I'm always chosen to play football and everyone knows I'm not stupid. My English is getting better every day and Marek is my best friend.

Miss Everard's Story

When Kwame first came to school he only spoke a little English. The other children didn't help him or spend time getting to know him. But he was so good and worked so hard, I didn't realise he was unhappy. I'm glad his mum and dad talked to me.

Kwame told the children about his school in Ghana, and they asked him lots of questions. Now they know more about him they have been kinder and more helpful.

WE ARE DIFFERENT AND THE SAME

All over the world, people speak different languages and look different from each other. They have different religions and cultures, but everyone belongs to the human race. Imagine how boring the world would be if we were all exactly the same.

By respecting and learning from each other we can live and work together happily and peacefully.

8

I'M LEFT OUT

Faiza is a Muslim. Most of her school friends are not Muslims. When they don't invite her to do things with them after school, she feels left out.

Ellie

Faiza

Ellie is Faiza's friend

Faiza is my new friend at school. We sat together at sports day yesterday. But my other friends say she's not allowed to have fun like us. Sometimes she wears different clothes to us. They say if we invite her to parties and sleepovers, she would spoil everything.

9

My school friends do things together after school, but they never ask me to join in.

When they talk about the fun they had, I feel left out. They say, "Oh you wouldn't enjoy it, Faiza. You're a Muslim."

They think, because I'm a Muslim, I'm not allowed to watch television or play computer games or listen to music. They think my mum and dad are very strict so they don't want to come to my house.

What can Faiza do?

It would help if Faiza's friends understood her religion better. She can:

★ tell her mum and dad what her friends think
★ tell her friends why she sometimes wears different clothes to them
★ say she wants to join in with them more.

what Faiza did

I talked to my mum and she talked to my teacher and to Ellie's mum. My teacher invited my mum to talk about our religion at school. Mum was shy but she was brilliant and everyone liked her. They understand us much better now.

Ellie's been round to my house and I've been round to hers. We had lots of fun!

WHAT IS RACISM?

Racism is treating someone differently, unfairly or unkindly just because they are different. There are all kinds of ways of being different. People have different coloured skin, speak different languages and have different religions and cultures.

Racism can be saying unkind things, leaving someone out, spoiling their things or hurting them.

Both children and adults may be racist. But, racism is a kind of bullying. It is never all right to be racist.

IT'S MY HOME TOO!

Dipti's dad comes from India but she was born in this country. She was shocked when someone told her to go back to where she came from.

Gemma

Dipti

Gemma is Dipti's friend

I was playing with Dipti when some kids in our class said, "Go back where you came from Dipti!"

I asked Dipti, "Where do you come from?"

She said, "Here! The same as you." Then she cried. I didn't mean to upset her.

13

My brother and I were born in this country, the same as Gemma. Then she asked where I came from because of what some kids at school said! I was really upset and cross with her. Just because I have different coloured skin they think this isn't my home. But it is!

Lauren's family come from France, but he was born here too. No one says, "Go back to where you came from!" to Lauren. I think that's because he has the same coloured skin as them.

What can Dipti do?

The children said a racist thing to Dipti. They didn't bother to find out about her - they thought they already knew her. She can:

* ★ tell Gemma why she's upset by her question
* ★ tell her teacher what the children said.

What Dipti did

I told Gemma why she upset me and she was really sorry. We're best friends again now. Gemma came with me to talk to our teacher.

Dipti's Family Tree

Grandma (Born India) Grandpa (Born India) Grandma (Born India) Grandpa (Born India)

Mum (Born UK) Dad (Born India)

My brother Ashok (Born UK) Me (Born UK)

Our teacher asked us all to make a family tree. We found that lots of us had parents and grandparents from all over the world, not just me!

CELEBRATIONS

A head teacher's story

Children in our school come from many different backgrounds. We learn about our different religions and respect each other's special celebrations.

Nativity play
(Christianity)

Christians celebrate the birth of Jesus at Christmas. At the same time of year, Jewish people light candles to celebrate Hanukkah and Hindus celebrate Divali, the festival of lights.

Muslims pray together at Friday prayers. Friday sunset to Saturday sunset is the Sabbath - Jewish holy day. Christians go to church on Sunday. It's nice to know we've got so many things to celebrate!

Inside a mosque
(Islam)

Josh's story

For my birthday, I planned a bowling party and a sleepover. All my friends said they would come - except David. He said. "I can't, it's the Sabbath."

We gave David a hard time about that!

I told my dad that David couldn't come - just because it's Sabbath!

But Dad explained that David is Jewish and that Sabbath is important in his religion. They have a family meal together on Friday nights. I felt bad about giving David a hard time.

Dad said, "We can go another night so David can come too." So we did and David came. I said sorry to David and we're friends again now.

The Sabbath
(Judaism)

RACISM IS MAKING MY FRIEND UNHAPPY

Reggie's friend Shen is being teased about his name. Reggie doesn't want his friend to be unhappy. He wants to do something to help him.

Reggie

Reggie is Shen's friend

My friend Shen's mum and dad are from China. He was born in the same hospital on the same day as me! We have joint birthday parties. We've always been friends and so have our mums.

Shen

"It's my name!"

Shen is a Chinese name.

Some children in our school started calling Shen lots of different names they thought sounded Chinese like Ching and Wong. They thought it was funny.

But Shen didn't laugh. He got angry.

I said to him, "It's only a name!"

But Shen said, "It's my name! I'm not just a Chinese boy. I'm me and my name is Shen!"

I can see what he means. My grandad's name is Reginald. I'm called after him and I'm proud of my name.

Making fun of Shen's Chinese name is a kind of racism. Reggie can help to stop it. He can:

★ try to imagine how Shen feels
★ tell Shen he understands and that he'll stand up for him and help stop the other children calling Shen the wrong names.

what Reggie did

When the children started calling Shen the wrong name, I told them it was unkind and they should stop. They just laughed and went on doing it. Shen and I pretended not to hear.

Shen never, ever answered to the wrong name. They soon got bored and stopped. Shen is much happier now.

20

I'M IN A GANG

Binh is in a gang. All his friends live in the same part of town and share the same culture. They are unfriendly to children who aren't the same as them.

Binh

Marvin is Binh's friend

Binh used to be my friend. He isn't friendly to me any more because he's in a gang that I'm not allowed to join. His gang think they're better than everyone else!

Marvin

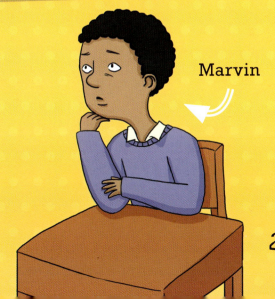

Binh's Story

I was proud to be in the gang. We all live near each other and our parents all come from Vietnam.

When Marvin wanted to do things with us, the gang wouldn't let him.

They said, "You're not one of us!" Then they said stuff about the colour of his skin and other unkind things.

Marvin didn't like that. I didn't like it either but I didn't say anything. I can't be in the gang and be Marvin's friend too.

What can Binh do?

Not letting someone join your gang because of where they come from or the colour of their skin is racism. He can:

★ think how Marvin feels
★ remember that Marvin was his friend first
★ ask himself if he wants to be in a gang.

What Binh did

I decided I didn't want to be in a gang if my best friend couldn't be in it too.

Marvin agreed with me and we just walked away. I felt good about that - and so did Marvin. We've made lots more friends too. Now we've stood up to the gang, maybe they'll stop behaving like racist bullies.

23

I'M SCARED

A gang is frightening Bilal and his little sister Nasreen. Nasreen wants to tell their mum and dad, but Bilal says she mustn't tell anyone.

Bilal

Nasreen

Nasreen's story

Every day after school, a gang waits for me and my brother on the way home. They steal our stuff and call us names. They say, "You don't belong here!"

Bilal says they'll do more bad things to us if we tell anyone.

Bilal's story

I feel really afraid of a gang of racist bullies. They push me and Nasreen and say bad things to us. If we have any money or anything they like the look of, they just steal it!

I want to tell someone, but they say they'll hurt Nasreen if I do.

So I made Nasreen promise not to tell. Now I think she's a bit scared of me as well. But it's my job to look after my little sister! I don't know what to do.

What can Bilal and Nasreen do?

They can't beat the bullies on their own but no one can help them if they don't say anything. They can:

★ make a diary of what the gang does every day
★ tell their parents or a grown-up they trust and show them the diary.

What Bilal did

I told our parents. They said, "We can't deal with this on our own."

They told the school and the police and the gang was punished.

An adult walks home with us every day. We feel safe now and the gang didn't win.

RACISM IN SCHOOLS

All schools have rules about racism.
Felicity had a lesson about it.

At school, our class discussed how racism hurts people. We agreed racism is always wrong and that we wouldn't do or say racist things.

If we see anyone being racist, even an adult, we must tell someone about it. Sometimes we can stop racism happening to us by standing up to the bullies. Or we can keep calm and walk away. But we often need help from a grown up.

Our school has strict rules about racism. Teachers or other members of staff will always help if we go to them.

27

WE DEALT WITH RACISM

Mel made racist comments about Aleesha when she first came to school. She tried to stop Aleesha making new friends.

Mel and Aleesha's story

Aleesha: I missed my friends at my old school but I thought I'd soon make new friends at my new school. I was getting on well, but then Mel started saying racist things about me!

Mel: When Aleesha first came to school, my friends thought she was really cool. They all wanted to be her friend. I was jealous so I said racist things to try and turn them against her. The racist comments worked! Some of my friends even joined in being unkind to Aleesha.

Aleesha: When I heard what Mel and her friends were saying about me, I was upset and angry. I wanted to shout at Mel but I thought, "That won't make the other children like me."

Mel: My plan was going well, until Sam said I shouldn't say racist things about Aleesha.

Aleesha: I didn't have to shout at Mel because Sam stood up for me. It was great!

Mel: I was angry and upset with Sam and I told him so. He said, "Now you know how Aleesha feels!" I hadn't thought about how Aleesha was feeling.

Aleesha: Mel's friends started being nice to me and being unkind to her! So now I felt sorry for her.

Mel: I decided to say sorry to Aleesha. I don't like saying sorry and it was difficult. But she was really cool about it.

Aleesha: Mel and I both know how it feels when someone makes racist comments. It isn't nice. I've made lots of new friends now and Mel is one of them!

GLOSSARY

Celebrations
A festival, party, meal or religious service held on a day that is special to a group of people or a religion.

Christian
Someone who is Christian follows the religion of Christianity.

Culture
The culture of a country is its art, music, ideas and beliefs.

Family tree
A family tree is a diagram shaped like a tree that shows how the members of a family are related to each other and when they were born.

Gang
A gang is a group of friends who go round together and play together.

Jewish
Someone who is Jewish follows the religion of Judaism.

Language
The language of a country is how the people speak. For example, the English language is spoken in England and Australia.

Muslim
A Muslim is a believer in the religion of Islam.

Race
A race is a group of people who come from the same part of the world.

Racism
Racism is when a person or group of people are treated badly because of their race.

Religion
A religion is a set of beliefs about god. Christianity, Islam, Hinduism, Sikhism, Judaism and Buddhism are all religions.

Sabbath
The Sabbath is a holy day of rest and worship in Judaism.

FURTHER INFORMATION

For children

www.childline.org.uk
Helpline: 0800 1111
Childline is a free helpline for children in the UK. You can talk to someone about any problem and they will help you to sort it out.

kidshealth.org/en/kids/bullies.html
Learn about bullies and how to deal with them.

www.kidscape.org.uk
A website helping to prevent racist bullying.

For parents

www.familylives.org.uk
Helpline for parents:
0808 800 2222
Family Lives offers advice, guidance and support for parents who are concerned about their children. The 'Bullying UK' section offers advice for parents whose children are being bullied at school.

For readers in Australia and New Zealand

kidshelpline.com.au
Online and phone help for a wide range of issues.

www.cyh.com
Loads of online information about all sorts of issues including racist bullying.

www.kidsline.org.nz
A helpline run by specially trained young volunteers to help kids and teens deal with troubling issues and problems.

INDEX

Notes for parents, carers and teachers

Children can experience racist bullying simply because they are different in some way. It might be because they belong to a different race or culture or because of their religion or even their accent. There are many ways parents, carers and teachers can help children deal with racism.

- Children need to know racism is always wrong.
- If a child is experiencing racism, it is not their fault.
- Building up a child's self-esteem is helpful.
- Fear of making things worse can stop children telling anyone. They need to know that the adult they tell will take effective action.

Page 5 Kwame's story

The children in Kwame's class have decided he is stupid because he's still learning to speak English.

- Children can be encouraged to get to know each other properly and not to make judgements about other children because they are different.

Page 10 Faiza's story

Faiza feels left out because her friends don't understand her religion even though they think they do.

- Understanding each other's religion and culture can help children to have fun together and respect any differences at the same time.

Page 14 Dipti's story

Dipti is upset because she has been told to "Go back where she came from!"

- Children should understand that this is a racist comment and that it is hurtful and upsetting and never acceptable.

Page 17 Josh's story

Josh was unkind to his friend because of his religion.

- It's kinder and more helpful to find a way round a difference than to create a conflict over it.

Page 18 Reggie's story

Reggie's friend is unhappy because he is being called the wrong name.

- Laughing at someone's name because it sounds foreign is upsetting. Calling someone by their proper name shows you respect them.

Page 22 Binh's story

Binh's gang is excluding Marvin because he isn't 'one of them'.

- Gangs based on race can lead to racist behaviour against other people. Children should be encouraged to include any child in their group of friends.

Page 25 Bilal's story

Nasreen and Bilal are being intimidated by a gang.

- This kind of racism needs effective intervention from an adult. Fear of walking to and from school can be a sign that children are being bullied.

Page 28 Playscript: Mel and Aleesha's story

Children could 'perform' the parts in this simple playscript. They could also write and perform their own play about racism.